TUCKY THE HUNTER

-to Frank Sutherland -
from
James Dickey

- Christmas, 1978 -

Other Books by the Authors

BY JAMES DICKEY

Buckdancer's Choice
Deliverance
Drowning with Others
God's Images: The Bible — a New Vision
Helmets
The Undead
The Zodiac

BY MARIE ANGEL

The Ark
The Art of Calligraphy: A Practical Guide
Beasts in Heraldry
The Twenty-third Psalm: King James Version
(illustrated)

TUCKY THE HUNTER

BY
JAMES DICKEY

ILLUSTRATED BY
MARIE ANGEL

CROWN JEWEL

CROWN PUBLISHERS, INC., NEW YORK

Printed in the United States of America

Published simultaneously in Canada by
General Publishing Company Limited

Library of Congress Cataloging in Publication Data

Dickey, James.
Tucky the hunter.

SUMMARY: A child hunts the animals of the world with
a pop-gun and the snare of his imagination.
[1. American poetry]   I. Angel, Marie. II. Title.
PS3554.I32   1978   811'.5'4   78-9343
ISBN 0-517-53258-1

TO
James Bayard Tuckerman Dickey
herein known as Tucky

TUCKY THE HUNTER

HE shot the two-horned rhino

with his double-barreled gun,

He shot the dusty python

for sleeping in the sun.

He shot the bullish elephant, the king of pachyderms,

He shot the bristling cougar, and fed him to the worms.

He shot the grinning crocodile in the Ganges thick and brown,

While he gobbled up a newsboy in the middle of the town.

LASKA knew his courage

whenever he came back,

For he'd shot the gruesome grizzly,

and the bumbling Kodiak.

He shot the mountainous King-Kong, whom everybody knows;

He was holding up a kicking girl, and pulling off her clothes.

HE SHOT the bearded barbary goat,

as it sat looking wise,

And, creeping into Eden,

shot the Bird of Paradise.

With his knife hung from his studded belt his double-barreled gun,

Tucky the Hunter hunted on, through the suburbs of the sun.

Where flamingos put the moon out,

then lay down in the weeds,

And night sprayed burning egrets

on the ever-swinging reeds,

Where the moon charged like a

red-eyed bull, then plunged into the sea,

Tucky hunted EVERYTHING—

but I hope not YOU and ME!

E SHOT the snapping wolverine,

just as it sallied forth;

His great gun bammed, and that was IT

for the Demon of the North.

He shot the one-eyed Yonghy, and then he bagged the Bo,

Then finished off the triple of the Yonghy-Bonghy-Bo.

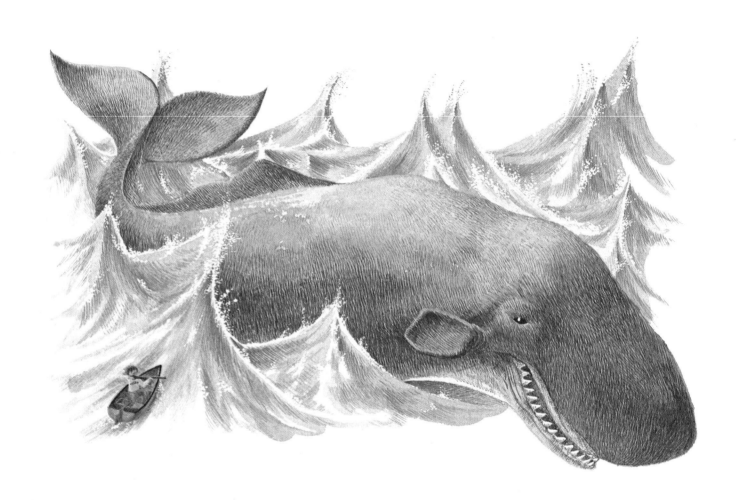

HE SHOT the native boomalong,

with its eye of night-shade blue;

And the yellow Malay monkey

for doing nasties in the zoo.

At Samarkand the whirling stars all whistle wild and pale,

And so they do off Durban, where Tucky shot the whale.

E SHOT the smiling Devil,

in flames of blow‑torch blue;

The angels came out dancing,

and Tucky shot them too.

Like clay pipes in a gallery, he shot the trembling stars,

He shot the burly Bintarong‑ but he NEVER shot at cars!

ND he shot EVERYTHING there was,

but they weren't really DEAD!

All summer, winter, spring and fall

he shot them in his bed.

FOR a pop-gun has strange powers,

and the animals know this:

It wounds with simple love alone,

with the tension of a kiss.

And when the pop-gun fires,

    a loving life for the bold

Is born in the heart of the hunter,

    a hunter five years old.

The animals would rise and wait

in tree-top and in den

And watch the West-red sun go down

so Tuck could hunt again.

When the real sun sank as the earth rolled, Tuck's O W N moon and H I S sun

Came out, and H E'D set out, with his knife and his double gun.

One night he started all alone for the coast of Palawan;

And shot the gristly Tiger-Shark and the ever-dying swan.

HE SHOT the scented meadow-lark;

he slew it for its song,

And put the song in his pocket

as he hunted right along,

And when his mother came for him, before the break of light,

She wondered where he'd got that song, so mournful and so right.

**S**HE wondered where he'd got that song,

that sounded like noon-flight;

She wondered where he'd got it,

in the middle of the night.

And the beasts all rose up singing, as she took Tuck in her arms,

And everything was banished that comes from night's alarms.

The animals and fish were there, and birds flew through the room;

There was nothing but Creation in night's suburban gloom.

And the beasts were glad to be there, that fell to Tucky's gun;

They were glad to be a part of that great nocturnal fun.

And they were grave and stately, but laughing with delight,

As Susan raised up Tucky in the middle of the night.

The hunt was almost over,

for Tuck was growing up,

And he'd never have any more to drink

from inspiration's cup.

**B**UT while he was a little child,

for a time that wouldn't last long,

He held within his pocket

the meadow-lark's light song.

And the animals rose up singing when Susan held him near

All the beasts that Tucky shot were seen both dear and clear:

ND his mother, Susan,

then most strangely began to sing

The song of the single meadow-lark,

and the song of the Cobra King:

HE sang of strange night-wonders,

    meant just for mother and son:

She sang as only a mother can sing

    to her one and only one,

ND the animals sang with her;

they sang of all the stars:

They sang on the streets of the suburbs

of Venus and of Mars:

They sang in mystic double-tongue, the tongue of man and beast,

They sang of Far West buffalo, and the jungles of the East,

ND SUSAN lay down singing,

very far from night's alarms.

His mother lay down singing

in Tucky's valiant arms.

JAMES DICKEY was born in Atlanta, Georgia, in 1923. He received his B.A. and M.A. degrees at Vanderbilt University where he matriculated in English, graduating Magna Cum Laude. During World War II and the Korean War he was a night fighter pilot, flying more than a hundred missions. For six years Dickey worked as an advertising executive in Atlanta and New York, writing poetry in the evenings. At the age of thirty-eight he won a Guggenheim Fellowship, withdrew from the advertising business, and began his career as a poet in earnest. Widely published in the major literary magazines of his day, Dickey's reputation as an important newcomer to American poetry grew rapidly. Between 1960 and 1966 he published four volumes of poetry, the last of which, *Buckdancer's Choice*, won the National Book Award. That same year he was appointed poetry consultant to the Library of Congress. In 1967 the publication of his collected works, *Poems 1957-1967*, was hailed as one of the literary events of the decade. His novel *Deliverance*, published in 1970, was a best seller. Two years later he wrote the highly successful screenplay for the film version of his book. Mr. Dickey is also the author of *The Suspect in Poetry*; *Babel to Byzantium*; *Self-Interviews*; *The Eyebeaters, Blood, Victory, Madness, Buckhead and Mercy*; *Sorties*; *Jericho: The South Beheld*; *The Zodiac*; and *God's Images*. In 1976 he was invited by incoming President Jimmy Carter to write and read an original poem for his inauguration. Out of this request came *The Strength of Fields*. Mr. Dickey has taught at Reed College, Rice University, and the Universities of Florida and Wisconsin. He has been Poet-in-Residence at the University of South Carolina for the past ten years. He is a member of the National Institute of Arts and Letters and the Academy of American Poets. He is married to his second wife, Deborah, and has two sons, Christopher and Kevin, and a grandson, Tucky.

MARIE ANGEL is a distinguished British artist who is best known for her calligraphy and her drawings of animals and flowers. She was educated at Coloma Convent and St. Anne's College and studied art at London's Croydon School of Art and the Design School of the Royal College of Art. Ms. Angel's artwork has been widely exhibited in England and the United States. She has illustrated works for private collections and limited editions; these include *A Bestiary* and *An Animated Alphabet*, published by Harvard College Library. Ms. Angel's drawings are in the permanent collections of the Hunt Botanical Library, the Harvard College Library, and the Victoria and Albert Museum. She is an associate of the Royal College of Art.

In 1968 Ms. Angel illustrated her first children's book, *We Went Looking* by Aileen Fisher. Since then she has done several others, including *The Tale of The Faithful Dove* and *The Tale of Tuppenny* by Beatrix Potter, and *The Ark, Beasts in Heraldry*, and *The Twenty-third Psalm*.

Ms. Angel lives in Warlingham, England, and enjoys gardening, sports cars, and her cats, who often appear in her illustrations.